Pukka

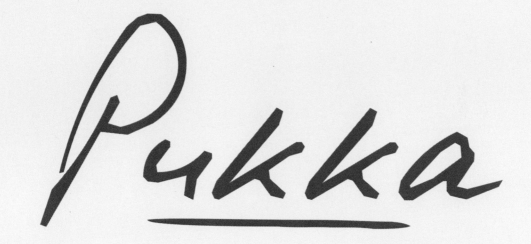

Pukka

THE PUP AFTER MERLE

AS TOLD BY PUKKA TO *Ted Kerasote*

Houghton Mifflin Harcourt
Boston • New York
2010

For information about permission to reproduce selections from this book, write to Permissions,
Houghton Mifflin Harcourt Publishing Company, 215 Park Avenue South, New York, New York 10003.

www.hmhbooks.com

Library of Congress Cataloging-in-Publication Data
Pukka : the pup after merle / as told by Pukka to Ted Kerasote.
p. cm.
ISBN 978-0-547-38608-9
1. Dogs—Anecdotes. 2. Human-animal relationships—Anecdotes. 3. Dog owners—Anecdotes.
I. Kerasote, Ted.
SF426.2.P85 2010
636.70092'9—dc22   2010005745

Printed in the United States of America

DOC 10 9 8 7 6 5 4 3 2 1

Photo credits appear on page 200.

This book is printed on FSC (Forest Stewardship Council)–certified stock

Old Christmas is past, twelve tide is the last
And we bid you adieu, great joy to the new.

—from "The King," Traditional English Carol

Pukka

Some of you may remember Merle and Ted from a book he wrote about their life in Wyoming. They shared a lot of adventures, and Ted missed Merle terribly when he died.

That's why Ted didn't get another dog right away. He spent a lot of time by himself, skiing in the mountains, as he and Merle had done, while he wrote Merle's story.

Then he traveled on Merle's book tour, meeting many other dogs and their people.

One day in Minnesota, he met my mom, Abby, and she reminded him of Merle. She was calm and even looked like Merle.

She had a litter of three-day-old pups, but Ted couldn't take one home with him because he was going to be traveling on Merle's book tour for a long time.

He never forgot my mom, though, and a year later she had another litter with my dad, Taylor.

My dad lives in Minnesota, too, and he and my mom knew each other, and liked each other a lot, before they had pups together.

A day after I was born, Ted flew to Minnesota and saw me.
I couldn't see him, though, because my eyes were still closed.

I guess he liked me and my brothers and sisters, because seven weeks later, there he was again, seeing us all grown up and ready for our new homes.

He did puppy aptitude tests with us.

And I was his favorite out of the litter. He thought that I was athletic . . .

and calm . . .

and affectionate.

He also said that he liked me because my face reminded him of Merle's.

After a while I got tired of puppy aptitude testing. It was a lot of work and not much play. So I showed Ted what I thought of all his notes!

He didn't mind. We hit it off, and he asked me if I wanted to come to Wyoming with him.

I wasn't sure where Wyoming was, or even what it was, but Ted smelled good, had a nice voice, and that elk jerky he gave me — mmm-mmm-mmm. If elk jerky came from Wyoming, I was ready to go.

I wasn't happy about leaving my mom and my Uncle Casey . . .

But Ted had a big soft pillow in his car just for me, and all sorts of interesting food and toys, and even a seat belt made for dogs that was just my size.

Interstate 90 went on forever—really boring!—so I caught a lot
of shut-eye.

Until we got to the motel. Then I was wide awake and ready to play.

And I couldn't believe it! There was another puppy in our room, and it looked just like one of my brothers!

We stayed in Rapid City, South Dakota, and Cooke City, Montana, and I got the motel scene down pretty quickly. At night Ted kept me in a little crate next to his bed, and all I had to do was whine, "I have to go. Right now, quick!" and up he'd jump—and out we'd run—so I could pee on the grass instead of in our room.

I think we were in Rapid City when Ted said, "You are quite the pukka dog. Do you know that?"

He told me that it was an old Hindi word that meant "genuine" or "first class," and it sounded like the puck used in hockey. He liked the word, he said, because he knew—after only three days—that I was both a genuine and first-class pup.

"What do you think of that name?" he asked me. "Will Pukka work for you?"

"Sounds good to me," I said, and closed my eyes.

The next day we went over a high pass in Wyoming and I saw my first snow. Ted seemed pretty excited about snow, but I wasn't so sure about it. It was cold on my paws!

From there we went down into Yellowstone National Park, where I smelled my first bison poop—now that was exciting!

Soon I got to see the bison themselves. They're huge, and I was glad to be in Ted's arms.

I also got to smell wolves. They're big dogs, and when I heard them howl it gave me the shivers.

I saw a moose,

and a black bear, who I thought was a big black dog until it came close to us.

Finally we saw a grizzly bear. It was a ways off . . .

When it came closer, I was happy to be in the car.

As we drove into Kelly the next day—that's where Merle and Ted lived, and it's now where I live—we saw a herd of elk right behind the house. Ted said this was a good omen, since he thought I'd probably like elk a lot.

By then I was really tired of the car and glad to get out of it—what a long way it is from Minnesota to Wyoming!

Right away some of Ted's friends came by to say hi. Bailey was first. She's a famous grouse hunter.

Next I met Goo, an English Setter, and A.J., a yellow Labrador Retriever like me. A.J. lives across the field and comes over to visit with Ted every day. He's almost like Ted's dog, and I thought he was going to be my best friend, too. But was I ever wrong!

We put our things away and walked over to Tessa and Eliza's house. Merle used to babysit Tessa when she was a little girl, but now Tessa's a teenager, and I guess Eliza is too, and they puppysit me.

Their dog's named Buck, and I *really* liked him. After one sniff, I thought, "Now here's a dog I can learn something from."

The next morning Ted went back to work because he was trying to finish a book, and I figured I'd better help him.

I found out, though, that it's not very exciting looking at a computer screen.
I started playing with the mouse and following the cursor around. That's
when Ted gave me my first elk bone. Okay—that bone was worth all the
time I spent in the car!

I was happily eating my bone when A.J. came through Merle's door, as he'd been doing for a couple of years. I was so excited to see him—my first visitor! But A.J. saw my bone, and he saw me in Ted's office, and he was so jealous that a new dog was in Ted's life that he bit me in the head. I screamed and peed, and there was a lot of blood.

Ted picked me up in his arms and carried me around the house—after getting rid of A.J.—and said that I was a brave dog. He got me cleaned up and took me to Merle's old vet, Theo Schuff, who said my eye would be fine, if Ted took care of it.

He did—every day—talking to me softly and making my eye feel better with hot compresses.

I was still pretty shook up, so Ted took me to the Kelly post office, where I met some nice girls who played with me. I was a lot happier.

Then he took me for walks where there weren't any big dogs, and I could feel safe.

When I got tired, he carried me in his arms, telling me how sorry he was that he hadn't been able to stop A.J. from biting me.

I gave him a kiss. It hadn't been his fault.

Ted also made sure I got lots of kisses from everyone we met, which made me feel really good.

And in a couple of days I was back to my old form, playing hard and thinking of how I would get even with A.J. someday!

In the meantime, I started to meet lots of puppies, because Ted says that young dogs should meet other dogs their own age so they can play together.

One of my favorite new friends was Jasper, an Australian Shepherd. We could play for hours.

Did we ever go at it! Playing like this is important for puppies because it teaches you how hard you can bite before your friends stop playing with you.

I also visited the Kelly School and even though the first-graders pulled my ears and tugged at my tail, I wasn't scared.

My family in Minnesota had two children, and they had friends, so I met lots of kids from the time I was a tiny pup.

The next thing I learned was how to walk on a leash so I could go into Jackson, where there are lots of cars. I even brought the leash to Ted and figured out how to walk on it right away.

As soon as I tugged, Ted didn't. Soon I stopped tugging. But Merle had it right. Who wants to wear a collar all the time? It itches!

We went to the bank, the pet store, the kayak store, the café, and the bookstore. These were fun, but the most fun was stopping at the Kelly post office to get the mail.

Some of Ted's friends, who had heard that he had a new dog, sent me packages, and Kathy the postmistress let me open them all by myself.

I loved showing off my new toys to everyone outside the post office, like Heather, who runs the café next door.

Ted and I also went to lots of parties during my first weeks in Wyoming—even big cocktail parties.

I was really good. I didn't jump on anyone and didn't pee on the rugs, but went outside as I'd been learning to do.

Like Ted says, though, "Life's not one endless party, Pukka. There are chores to get done around here."

First Ted did the irrigation, and of course I helped. Chewing on those hoses made my teeth feel good, and it didn't seem like a chore at all.

When we turned on the hose, what a surprise! I found out that water isn't solid. But it's still fun to chase.

Not long after we got done with the irrigation, Thekla came by with her horses Max and Jura.

I liked them a lot. Horses are as big as moose, but they're friendly—at least hers are.

The best part of meeting Max and Jura was that I got to play in the mud and become a really dirty dog for a change.

I needed a shower after that, which was no problem. I love getting in the shower with Ted. It's warm!

The next day we drove over to Idaho and I met June Bug, an expert retriever who showed me how to do it.

I could retrieve in just a little bit, but I think Merle was right: It gets boring after about four times.

We also went canoeing on the Snake River between Yellowstone and Grand Teton national parks so I could get used to water. First we had to put together the canoe, and I helped while wearing my new life preserver.

Since I'd already learned that water isn't solid, I made sure not to jump out.

On the lake shore where we landed, I met another puppy, a blue Heeler named Riley. I had a much better time playing with him than canoeing!

Each morning I went to school, and I still do. School isn't that bad, because when I get something right—like sitting, lying down, staying, or coming—I get a salmon treat.

And every few days Ted weighs me so he can give me the right amount of food. He wants me to grow, but not too fast. "We don't want you to have joint problems later on, Pukka," he tells me.

I give him a lick and say, "Just put more food in my bowl."

The hardest part of my life is when I get done eating and I have to watch Ted cook his own breakfast.

I don't understand why dogs have to stay out of the kitchen. That's where the best smells are! But that's one of the rules here. Sigh.

After breakfast we often walk around Kelly and stop by Buck's house to see if he wants to go with us. He always wants to go, and I follow him, smelling everywhere he smells.

And if something scares me, he says, "Now don't you worry, Pukka. I can take care of everything."

We often see Boone, who knew Merle when they were both young. She's very old now and can't hear at all, but she can still smell perfectly.

When we get back to our house, I like to lie by Merle's aspen tree, where he spent his last days, and when Ted sees me there he gets a faraway look in his eye.

I also learned how to go in and out of our house using Merle's door. It was a snap. Then one day we went over to Ted and Merle's old trailer so Ted could show me where he and Merle began, and I used Merle's door there, too.

I went back and forth—it was a lot of fun, smelling Merle and Gray Cat and their friends—and Ted got that faraway look in his eye again, for no reason that I could understand.

Soon I could pee and poop outside all by myself.

Though when it was raining I sometimes made a mistake and did it in the house. Ted would pick me up and rush me outside, crying, "Outside! Outside!"

Sigh. Peeing in the rain isn't my favorite thing. It's so wet and yucky!

Even colder is snow—it can snow in Jackson Hole in June! We built fires, and let me tell you: After you have to pee outside in the cold, there's nothing better than relaxing in front of the wood stove.

What a surprise it was for Ted, though, when one night I decided not to come up to our bedroom.

"Are you going to sleep here in the living room?" he asked.

I was by the fire and gave a big stretch. "Yep," I said. "It's too comfortable to move."

"Suit yourself," he said, and after saying good night, he went up to our bedroom by himself.

I didn't go up until the next morning, and then I gave Ted another surprise, because I was watching him as he woke up.

"Good morning, Pukka," he said. "You seem to have things well under control."

"I do," I told him. "Merle wasn't the only freethinking dog, you know."

In three weeks my eye was much better, though I think I might always have a scar. That's okay. It'll remind me that a dog has to be careful, and life's not perfect.

But Ted thinks I'm perfect, which is one of the things I like about him. He's always saying, "You're the perfect puppy!" and "You're the best!" That's when I run to him as fast as I can.

He even thinks I'm perfect after I shred paper in his office . . .

And chew his shoes, which smell so good! He'll say, "Please give me that shoe,
Pukka." And I do because lots of times he gives me something else that I
really like—one of the elk bones we keep in the freezer. I have a lot of chew
toys, but therc is nothing better than a real bone!

The other thing I like about living with Ted is that he lets me decide things for myself—not everything, but lots of things. For instance, after I could hold my pee all night, he put a big round bed next to my crate and said, "Your choice, Pukka."

I went into the crate and gave it another try, but I preferred the bed since I could see all around me. I like that—a view—since a dog needs to keep track of things, even at night. So the bed it was and still is!

Soon I had my old confidence back. I had walked around Kelly, Jackson, and even the big city of Idaho Falls, meeting dozens of dogs and all sorts of people. I even taught Bruce, who can be a tough guy, how to walk politely on a leash.

That A.J., though! What a grouch! He wouldn't stop being mean to me. No matter how much I tried to be friends with him, he'd growl at me, pin his ears back, and keep his tail straight up in the air.

I might have given up, but I didn't. Since we lived just across the field from each other, we were going to have to be neighbors. Every day, I'd go over to play ball with him and the other dogs and Eric, their person. He's a great ball thrower.

I wish you could have seen A.J.'s face on the day I stole his ball from under his nose. He looked up at Ted, who was standing nearby, and said, "Didn't I beat up this little monster a few weeks ago? Do something! Get my ball back!"

"Sorry, A.J.," Ted told him. "You have to share—both the ball and me."

On many days people stop by our house to visit Merle's grave under the prayer flags. He was a really famous dog, and they leave flowers and note cards and little gold elk on top of where he's buried.

I go out to say hello to them, and I've gotten to meet people from all over the world. Many of them tell me, "Pukka, you've got some big paws to fill." But I'm not worried. Merle followed his nose, and I'll follow mine.

All these visits and school and walks tucker me out. I'm still a growing puppy and need lots of sleep. But after a little nap I'm ready to go again.

Hunting flies . . .

Watching deer from the dedicated quadruped couch . . .

Running through the arrowleaf balsam root . . .

Visiting Eliza . . .

Learning to retrieve, which is actually more fun than I thought it would be—at least for about six times . . .

Running with the other Kelly dogs . . .

And playing with Merle's prayer flags when they blow down in the wind. I can't decide which is more fun: shredding paper or chasing Merle's flags or playing with other dogs. Since I get to do all three, who cares!

Ted says it's hard to believe I've grown so big in just one month and have learned so much. I guess I am bigger. But I'm still a puppy, with lots to learn.

One of the most important things we've worked on during our second month together is having a gentle mouth. If I bite too hard, Ted will yell, "Ouch! That hurts!"

I got the idea pretty quickly—no hard biting—and he can now put his fingers, or even his nose, in my mouth and say, "Gentle, Pukka, gentle," and I'll just give him a little squeeze.

Another lesson I've learned is to help carry kindling into the house. But this doesn't seem like a lesson at all, because I love carrying sticks!

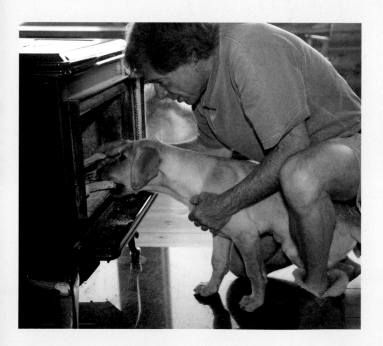

It's even more fun when I get to put the kindling into the stove myself and then watch Ted light the fire.

Once the fire's going, it's time to dance. "What'll it be this morning, Pukka?"
Ted asks me. "That's easy," I tell him. "Something bluegrass."

And off we go. Within a few weeks I could dance forward and backward, do turns, and zip through Ted's legs.

Of course, there are many harder things to learn. "Leave it" is the very hardest, especially when I'm starving and Ted has just filled my bowl with food.

But he says that learning "leave it" will stand me in good stead when I pick up something bad for me and he calls out, "Leave it!"

My other hard lesson is "wait." Ted makes it even harder by hiding around a corner of the hallway so I can't see him. I'm getting better at it, though.

"Thirty whole seconds," Ted says happily. "What a champ you are!" I don't know exactly how long thirty seconds is, but I tell you, it's a long time.

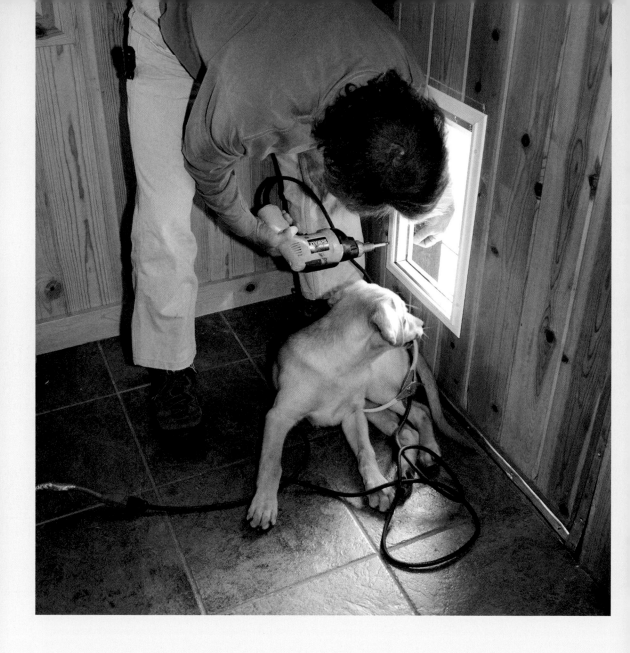

After our morning's lessons we sometimes get to do something fun instead of Ted going to work right away at his desk. One day we put in a new dog door since Merle's door was so old and the flap was torn from having been used so much. That Merle, now there was a dog who liked to go in and out.

I got to hold the pliers for Ted, and when we were done, he said, "Well, there it is, my friend. Merle's door is now Pukka's door."

In the afternoons we often go to town. Personally, I think we go into Jackson way too much, but Ted has lots of errands to run.

I like the car ride, but once we get there I have to wear my collar and walk on a leash. It's okay, but I sure prefer walking on my own, as we do in Kelly.

Ted also works at the Internet café, and I have to wait until he's done. He tells me, "Be patient, Pukka, and we'll have a nice walk when we get home."

I am patient, and when we get back to Kelly we always go for our walk, passing by the school, where Ted has taught me to go down a slide.

At first I was a little scared. The slide was slippery and it looked like a long way down to the ground.

Within a day, though, I was running to the top and leaping down the slide as fast as I could.

Soon we began to go on longer and more exciting walks, farther from Kelly and into the deep woods, where I learned to walk on logs. "Here we are," Ted would tell me, "in nature's agility course."

Everything has been so new on these walks that I have to stop often and smell. Ted never says, "Let's keep moving, Pukka." He waits as I take in all the new scents, and he'll teach me the names of what I'm smelling, saying, "That's a sticky geranium, Pukka," or "That's coyote poop," or "That's a wild rose."

I know a lot of words now. Among animal poop my favorite name is *elk* because I get to eat it at home—not the poop, but the meat. Among flowers, it's *wild rose*. Not only do roses smell good, but they're also tasty! Who would have thought that a flower could taste so sweet? But it does, and I eat as many as I can.

We had lots of rain in May, and it made the grass tall. I love standing in it up to my belly and looking out at the world.

I also love to run through it. I can run all day in the grass, and sometimes I do. Well . . . almost.

After a couple hours of walking and running and smelling, I'm a little tired. If we've taken the Subaru to the trailhead, I curl up on my bed in the back, with my blanket to cushion my head.

I also have my favorite yak chew toy and some bones, just in case I need to gnaw on something. And before we're home, I'm fast asleep.

I was having such a great time, playing and learning new things, but then one day, running along the irrigation ditch, I slipped and fell in the water.

Ugh! I was wet and cold again, just like when I was a small puppy and had to go outside to pee in the rain.

No matter what Ted did after that, he couldn't get me to go into the water. We even visited Ted's friend Mayo, who's trained lots of water dogs, and Mayo tried to lure me into the water with a stick and nice words about how much fun it would be, but I wasn't convinced.

Then Ted tried something different. He took me to a wide shallow stream and crossed it. Instead of stopping at the other side, he just kept walking. I whined and cried out, "Come back! Don't leave me!" But he kept going.

So I jumped in and raced across the water, trying hard not to touch it. And do you know what? The stream was warm! It came from a hot spring. Warm water! What a great idea—like our shower—and much better than cold water. I didn't want to get out.

The next day Ted went to another stream and started to walk across it. I followed him and the water was a little colder than the day before, but not by much. Suddenly, I couldn't think about whether the water was warm or cold. My paws weren't on the bottom! That was scary, and I started moving them, almost like I was walking, except I was floating.

What a great moment this was—water's not solid, but I could still cross it! Ted turned around and said, "Guess what, Pukka? You're swimming!" And just like that, I was.

Right after my first swim Ted took me to a nearby slough and threw my retriever dummy across it. I can't explain what happened next. But something said *yes* in my head. I jumped in, swam across, and brought the dummy back to Ted. It was as easy as one, two, three.

"Pukka!" Ted exclaimed, giving me a treat. "I think your genes are kicking in."

Everything seemed less hard after I learned how to swim. We went back to the Kelly School playground and Ted said, "There are big mountains around here, Pukka, so you may want to learn to climb." Ted went up the ladder, and I went up after him.

We also climbed up to a bigger slide—a tube—and Ted went in first, calling to me, "I'm right here, Pukka. No worries—come on down." I didn't want to go at first, but Ted climbed back up, held me in his arms, and we slid down together.

Wow! Was that ever fun!

After that, Ted couldn't keep me out of the slides. I loved all the tubes, but the biggest one was my favorite. I loved diving into it head first . . .

. . . and coming out the other end—all by myself.

June became July, the summer got warmer, and I got bigger. Ted and I walked all around Kelly, and I learned the trails and the rivers and the hills. Sometimes we started our walk as the sun rose, and that was one of my favorite times of the day.

The air was still, and there were lots of smells heavy on the ground from the animals who came by in the night. Opening my mouth, I took them all in.

Sometimes we went out in the afternoons, walking along the hills above Kelly. This was a good time, too. The warm wind blew through the grass and brought smells from far away.

And sometimes we went to where the lupine was blooming, making the world smell sweet.

Every day—or almost every day—I played with my dog friends. Willie, an English Setter, was a lot bigger than me, but still played with me like a puppy.

We also visited Bailey. She lives on a pond and taught me the finer points of retrieving. I showed her how to dance.

And of course there was Buck, who took me to some of his secret swimming spots.

Along the way, I found bones that Ted hadn't given me, and these became my favorite bones because I discovered them myself. Like this one. I ate it for weeks and weeks, until there wasn't a single bit of it left.

I also got to meet some new animals during this time. This baby robin fell out of its nest, and I ran to it. Ted yelled, "Leave it!" and I stopped short and just watched it.

"Well done!" Ted cried. That made me feel good, even though I wanted to catch the robin. Then Ted put the robin back with its mom, who was squawking at us.

One day I also met a mule deer along the river. I wasn't sure what to do about him—he was pretty big—so I looked at Ted, and he said, "Easy, Pukka. Steady. No chasing." So I stayed put.

Not long after that I got to meet my first cows. They seemed interested in me when we touched noses, but if I tried to play with them they put their heads down and tried to hook me with their horns. I decided that dogs are more fun to play with than cows—and safer!

Summer is also a time for parties, and croquet became one of my favorite games. There's a ball and a hammer and kids. They hit the ball and I run after it. Nothing could be better!

Well . . . there's one thing that's better—grilling buffalo burgers! And if I surprise the person grilling them, a burger may fall off the plate and into my mouth.

There are lots of different people at these parties, and you know what? I often go to the women first. This is because I've met men who slap me hard when they pet me or turn me over and hold me down when all I've done is try to make friends with them.

I don't understand why they do this. My mother never did this to me, and Ted never does this to me, and I've never met a woman who handles me roughly either. That's why I've become careful and go to the women first.

Of course, there have been a few bumps in the road during the summer, as Ted likes to say. Toilet paper has been one of them. It's just so delicious to chew on!

Another little bump has been during meals. I just can't stay away from the table, especially when the table is low and it's outside. Shouldn't low tables outside be for dogs?

So Ted leashes me to a tree and I have to sit and watch him and his friends eat until I learn not to bother them. Talk about hard!

I've tried to make up for being naughty by carrying my bowl to the sink so Ted can wash it. I don't know why he needs to wash it. I lick it clean!

There's one thing I do really well because Ted and I have worked on it a lot. I come with no more than a hand signal, or, if I'm out of sight, at his whistle.

When we practiced this and I came right away, he gave me elk jerky or smoked salmon and he'd cry out, "Excellent, Pukka! Well done! You're simply the best!" Then he'd give me a hug and my heart would fill with joy.

Then one day—I don't know exactly when it happened—rodents started to catch my attention. As we were walking along a trail, I heard a chipmunk squeak, and in the blink of an eye I knew I had to stalk and catch it.

The day before, chipmunks and squirrels meant nothing to me. The next day they were the most exciting animals in the world! Go figure.

And let me tell you: There is nothing—nothing!—better than leaping over the sagebrush after a ground squirrel.

Well . . . maybe there is. A few days later the very same thing happened when I smelled a grouse. I had smelled grouse before, and—what can I say?—they were just another bird.

Then, on this day I smelled a grouse and something went off in my brain. "Whoa!" that smell told me. "Get that grouse!" And the next moment I was flushing it. So I can't say if squirrels or grouse are more fun. I'm glad I don't have to choose!

Soon after I flushed my first grouse Ted and I were walking on the Coyote Rock trail and came to its high point, which overlooks the Tetons and Jackson Hole. We had been there once before—I remembered the trail because we had seen some elk up there—but this time I stopped dead in my tracks.

I had never thought that the world could be so big! I stared and stared from one end of the valley to the other, taking it in as if I could suddenly see space when before I couldn't. "Pukka," said Ted, "I think you just noticed distance." And I had.

It was during this time that Ted wanted to run more rivers, and he thought that I'd be happier on a cataraft than in a canoe, because I could sit comfortably on the deck he built for me and watch the scenery go by.

We saw some beautiful country on our floats.

And we ran some exciting rapids, though I was never worried since Ted was right there, saying "Wow, Pukka, for a dog who didn't like water, you sure have made a turnaround."

I had. Water wasn't yucky anymore. But as much as I liked water, I was happier when we were back on land and I could stretch my legs and take a walk.

Soon we were doing some long ones. One of the very best was our hike to Jackson Peak when I was five months old. This is about the age, Ted told me, that wolf pups leave their den and begin to travel with their parents. "Pukka," he said, "I think you're ready for an overnighter."

We followed a trail that went through big trees, and I smelled black bear, elk, deer, and I don't know how many squirrels. The squirrels were the most fun because I'm allowed to chase them.

At the end of the trail we reached Goodwin Lake, and Ted climbed one of the shoreline rocks, but it was too steep for me. That made me sad, not being able to get up there with him.

I was much happier when we fetched water together. Except for chasing squirrels and grouse, and playing with my dog friends, and exploring in the fields around the house, I like doing most things with Ted.

After getting water we made camp and Ted fed me first, as he always does. Then we sat on the ground together, talking about our climb, until it got dark.

We got under our tarp and went to sleep side by side. Ted put his down parka over me, and it was just like a sleeping bag—very comfy.

As I fell asleep, I thought, "I like camping so much. Both people and dogs are at the same level—they sit on the ground, they eat on the ground, and they sleep on the ground, together. That makes a dog feel good! You can look people right in the eye; at home and in town, you're always looking up at them."

The next morning we got up while the stars were still out. We ate breakfast by headlamp and were on the ridge of Jackson Peak as the sun rose.

Up there I met a new animal called a pika. It lives in the rocks on high mountains, makes a little squeak, and is so much fun to chase.

But like squirrels and chipmunks, pikas seem impossible to catch . . . at least for now. I'm still trying!

I thought the world was big when I saw it from the top of Coyote Rock, but
was I ever wrong. It was even bigger from Jackson Peak. In fact, it was so big,
I had to sit down and just watch it.

By midmorning there was no place left to go. We had reached the summit. "Congratulations, Pukka," said Ted. "Your first mountain, almost eleven thousand feet, and just five months old!"

I felt terrific, like I was on top of the world. And we were.

On the way down I found out something about climbing mountains. Sometimes it's harder to go down than to go up. Ted had to give me a hand in one tricky spot, but that's all the help I needed.

Down, down, down we went, hiking into the afternoon, and when we got out of the trees and I looked back, whoa, was it ever a long way up there to the top of Jackson Peak! I couldn't believe we had been standing there that morning.

The moment we got to the trailhead, I jumped into our Subaru, lay down, and thought, "I just climbed a mountain!" Then I closed my eyes and fell asleep.

Ted had to get back to work the next day. He works too much, I think, as most people do. I lay on the deck, resting and making sure that no one would surprise him while he was in his office.

In the afternoon we walked to the post office, and I told Kathy the postmistress all about Jackson Peak. She said, "Pukka, you got so big while you were gone. Pretty soon you won't be able to get up on the counter."

It was hot during these days, so I swam with Buck and Eliza in the Gros Ventre River.

And I saw Marybeth Minter, my other vet, who gave me my last vaccination and listened to my heart. I had to lie very still.

On one of my walks around Kelly I met a mother moose and her calf. Ted didn't even have to say "Easy, Pukka, steady." I just stood where I was and watched them. You don't want to mess with moose.

On a lot of days when Ted should have been writing, he told me about the vacation he wanted to take on the Main Fork of the Salmon River in Idaho with his old friend Bill.

"Think of it, Pukka," he'd say. "The River of No Return—warm water, sandy beaches, exciting rapids! Two whole weeks with no phone or e-mail! Bill and I have had many excellent adventures over the years, and now we'll have one with you."

I wasn't so sure that this was going to be an excellent adventure. Ted and Bill packed river gear for days — I watched them from the balcony above the living room.

And I could see that they were taking the cataraft. I knew what that meant — lots of floating and no hiking.

I was right, and it was even worse than I thought. We had to drive half a day to get to Salmon, Idaho, and then we had to stay in a motel, where I had to be on a leash as soon as I walked out of the room.

Even when we got to the boat ramp and were ready to launch, I had to stay in the car because that's what the Forest Service says dogs have to do.

By the time we had all our gear loaded on the raft and were ready to set off, I didn't want to go river running. I wanted to go for a long hike. So I jumped ashore when Ted wasn't looking.

He coaxed me back aboard with some salmon treats—I'm such a sucker for them—and telling me how much fun I'd have. So down the Salmon I went.

It was pretty, I have to admit, with tall mountains and white sandy beaches to run on — except they weren't big enough for a puppy with lots of energy.

For me the best part of each day was getting off the raft and scouting the rapids. It was another one of nature's agility courses.

Running with my retriever dummy when we got to camp also helped me feel less cooped up.

And so did swimming with Ted in the river, which was *really* warm.

Or at least some of the time it was. The weather got nasty for a day and a half, and it rained hard.

I was cold because I only had my puppy fur, but Ted gave me my own foul-weather gear, just like his and Bill's, and I felt much better.

Then the big rapids began, and let me tell you: They got my attention. There were waves that came over my head and Ted's, too.

We ran so many rapids that after a while I just sat there and watched them go by.

And within a few days I could see why people call this the River of No Return. I was wondering if we'd ever get home...or at least do something more interesting.

Finally, we did. We stayed at the same camp for two days and took a hike up a side valley. This was just what I needed.

That hike set me to thinking. Hiking was what I really wanted to do. So when we stopped at a place where people buy supplies, I had a little talk with Ted. I told him that I was tired of the river and didn't want to do any more rafting.

"What do you want to do, Pukka?" he asked me.

"I want to hike!" I said. "I want to be in the mountains again, like on Jackson Peak! I want to walk all day."

And that's exactly what Ted did for me. He cut the river trip in half, and we took a backpack in the Gros Ventre Mountains near Kelly. I was so happy, I was jumping for joy.

"Thank you!" I told Ted. "Thank you for listening to me."
    "Hey," he said, "we're in this together."

We saw many mountains during that week and camped by lakes and climbed Crystal Peak, where we could look all the way back to the Tetons.

The only hard part of the trip was that it was really cold in the mornings. Way below freezing! But Ted kept me in his sleeping bag until the sun came out.

We walked every day, and I didn't mind it a bit, because that's exactly what I wanted to do. And when we got back to the car, I thanked Ted again.

Back in Kelly, I washed off the trail dust in the sprinklers. I loved sprinklers when I was a little puppy, and I still love them. They're like a shower outside!

Once I shook myself off, I caught up on my bones . . .

Romped with Goo, who, like me, still has lots of puppy energy . . .

and went over to the Kelly School, where I played with the children.

It seemed as though we weren't home for very long when Ted said, "Pukka, I need to go to Seattle for a book signing, and it might be good for you to see what a big city is like. You do want to be a dog of the world, don't you?"

His voice sounded excited, and since he wasn't packing river gear, I figured, Why not? We were off on another adventure, and it was very different from the other ones we had been on, with lots of strange and interesting smells.

I learned to do some new things, too, like riding on an escalator. These are funny stairs that move up and down, and I raced them to the top.

I also watched Ted sign Merle's books.

And when he was done, we drove over to Pike Place Market. I could have spent the whole day there! There were dozens of nice people, and they gave me free samples of clover honey and blackberry jam and cheese.

These were good, but my favorites were the teriyaki jerky and the smoked sturgeon.

I saw a lot of strange animals at the market, like monkfish and crabs, but the strangest animal I saw was a bronze pig. I thought it was real . . . until I smelled it!

Seattle was fun—so many new smells and sights and people—but you can't pee and poop anyplace you want. And all that leash time! Life in the city is sure different from our life in Kelly. I was happy when Ted said, "Okay, Pukka, time to keep that promise I made to you about seeing the ocean."

We drove to Oregon, and when we got out of the car I could hardly take it all in. Talk about smells! And there was nothing at the end of the water—no mountains, no trees, no buildings. It was like the biggest lake in the world, except it tasted horrible when I tried to drink it.

At first the surf was scary, because it tried to drag me away. But Ted and I ran along it for a while and I got to understand how the ocean goes in and out, and how, if you time it right, you won't get dragged away.

Pretty soon I could hardly stay out of the surf. The beach—an ocean beach, not a river's beach—is a place where a dog can really run!

And jump!

And play!

I found out that I like the ocean as much as I like the mountains, although I did miss smelling all the big animals we have at home, like elk and bison and moose.

Still, I wouldn't mind coming back to the coast, and I asked Ted when we would. "Soon," he said. "But for now it's time to go back to Wyoming."

When we got home—surprise! The summer was over and the colors were changing.

The air was full of new smells, and it made me very excited about finding birds. Watching me run through the woods, Ted asked me, "Do you want to go bird hunting, Pukka?" I jumped up and licked his face and shouted, "I do! I really do!"

So off we went, and on my very first day I flushed seven pheasants and caught a rabbit all by myself. I ate every bit of the rabbit, except some of the fur, and when we got home I got to eat the pheasants, too.

We also went elk hunting. I love elk. It's better than rabbit, pheasant, or any dog food I've tried. It's the best! So I smell and listen and watch for the elk, and tell Ted where they are.

We haven't gotten an elk yet, but I sure hope we do, since I'm eating a lot now!

Ted weighed me the other day, and I was fifty-two pounds. "Wow, Pukka," he said. "Whatever happened to that little roly-poly puppy who came back with me from Minnesota?"

"I grew up," I told him. "And I'm still growing."

Part of growing up feels strange. So many things that used to interest me when I was a little puppy—like chewing shoes and people's hands and chasing butterflies—don't interest me anymore. But animals like squirrels and pheasants and elk fill my dreams, and I yip in my sleep as I chase them.

One thing from my puppy days that I don't think I'll ever forget, or will ever go away, is the scar under my eye that A.J. gave me. Oh, well. There are worse things that can happen to a dog.

What's funny, though, is that after all of A.J.'s grouchiness, he and I have finally become friends. Maybe it's because I'm as tall as he is, or maybe he realized that if he wanted to be friends with Ted he had to be friends with me.

Most of all I'm enjoying being home after all our travels. I like to lie on our deck and look at the Tetons from under Merle's aspen tree, as he used to do. I know why he liked it so much. It has a great view and lets a dog think. I think about all the places I've been and all the things I still want to learn. Like skiing. Ted says that soon it will snow and we'll be skiing. I can't even imagine what that is, but it sounds better than rafting, and I'm excited about it.

What an adventure being a puppy has been! I'm still a puppy—just six months old—but I'm on my way to being a dog. I've learned how to sit and lie down, how to heel and come. I know not to bother people while they're eating, and I can find my own way home. I leave shoes and toilet paper alone. I know the names of all the animals who live around us, and whom I can chase and whom I can't. Best of all—and I don't know how I learned this, since we never practiced it—I feel like Ted and I are a team. He shows me things I haven't seen; I show him things he can't hear or smell. He stands by me; I stand by him.

This is such a great time—sometimes being a puppy, sometimes a dog—and . . . right now . . . I'm feeling puppyish. I need a little nap, and then I'll be ready for whatever comes my way.

See you then!
Pukka

Pukka and Ted send many thanks to

Kim Fadiman, as always, for reading our words, sharing our river trips, and listening with such enthusiasm to our stories.

April North for following the growth of our story from its start, for many puppy walks, and for being the best of friends.

The Landale family for puppysitting and for reading our first installments.

Elpis Kerasote and the Rallis family for listening to the first parts of our story.

Pam Poon, Robin Houston, Ralph Yaeger, and Peter, Anthony, and Raymond Vasilas for reading the entire manuscript.

Dina Sutin and Allison von Maur for their help in choosing a cover.

Bill Liske for his editorial advice and putting up with us for such a very long time.

And Laurie Brown and Andrea Schulz for being such great supporters.

I, Pukka, would also like especially to thank and remember June Bug, who first taught me to retrieve, who played with me when other big dogs wouldn't, and who shared every one of her toys. Too soon gone.

June Bug

July 8, 2005–November 21, 2009

About the Photographs

Living with Pukka every day, I, Ted, took most of the images in this book. Occasionally, I handed the camera off to someone standing nearby and asked him or her to photograph Pukka and me. The photographs that were taken in this way are labeled HO (handed off) in the credits below.

Three photographers also accompanied Pukka and me on some of our adventures and captured what we were doing. They were Baker Rawlings of Bellevue, Washington; Bill Liske of Ridgway, Colorado; and Heather Erson of Jackson Hole, Wyoming (heathererson.com).

Most of my photographs were made with a Nikon D300 camera and Nikon 18–200mm lens. I also used a Canon Power Shot SD870IS Digital Elph and a Canon Vixia HF20 camcorder off of which I pulled a few stills. Bill Liske also used a Nikon D300 and Nikon 18–200mm lens, along with a Nikon 12–24mm lens. Heather Erson used a Canon 5D camera and the following Canon EF lenses: 17–40mm, 24–105mm, and 70–200mm. Baker Rawlings used a Nikon D700 camera with a Nikon 28–105mm lens.

All the digital images were edited in Adobe Bridge and Photoshop by myself and Eric Rohr of Jackson Hole, and the layout was a team effort between George Restrepo of Houghton Mifflin Harcourt in Boston, Andrea Schulz of Houghton Mifflin Harcourt in New York, and myself in Jackson Hole.

Photo Credits

Cover, 4–6, 8, 10, 11 (top), 13, 15–24, 25 (top left, bottom left, bottom right), 26–27, 28 (bottom), 29–33, 35, 39, 41–51, 53–54, 57, 66–69, 72–87, 97–109, 110 (top), 111–134, 145 (main image), 146, 151–157, 161, 163, 165, 168, 174, 176–179, 185–186, 193–196: *Ted Kerasote*

1: *Allison von Maur (HO)*

2: *Lou Dawson*

3: *Harvey Finkel*

7, 9, 11 (bottom), 14: *Doug Radloff (HO)*

12: *Tessa Landale (HO)*

25 (bottom left): *Liz Gilliam (HO)*

28 (top), 38: *Steve Sharkey (HO)*

34, 52, 55, 58–65, 70–71, 88–96, 135–144, 145 (inset), 147-150, authors' photo: © *Heather Erson*

36-37, 56: *April North (HO)*

40: *Bob Ciulla (HO)*

110 (bottom): *Bev Boynton (HO)*

158–160, 162, 164, 166–167, 169–173, 175, 187–192: *Bill Liske*

180–184: *Baker Rawlings*

199: *Susan Lykes*